"As a therapist in the field of neurodiversity for nearly two decades and a neurodivergent adult, I find Daniel Jones' work inspiring and refreshing. His content is not only informative and educational but also relatable and entertaining. He provides a unique perspective on life as a neurodivergent individual, and his advocacy for this community is commendable. I highly recommend his channel, books, and courses to anyone looking to learn more about autism and neurodiversity."

—*Karla Pretorius*, MA in Psychology

An Approachable Guide to
Living Excellently on the Spectrum

Autism
for
Adults

Daniel M. Jones

PAGE STREET
PUBLISHING CO.

PAGE STREET
PUBLISHING CO.

First published in 2023 by
Page Street Publishing Co.
27 Congress Street, Suite 1511
Salem, MA 01970
www.pagestreetpublishing.com

Distributed by Macmillan, sales in Canada by The Canadian Manda Group.

27   26   25   24   23   1   2   3   4   5

ISBN-13: 978-1-64567-887-8
ISBN-10: 1-64567-887-3

Library of Congress Control Number: 2022948029

Cover and book design by Molly Kate Young for Page Street Publishing Co.

Printed and bound in China

I would like to dedicate this book to my followers and supporters from all over the world; without you, I would not be doing this, and this book would not be a thing.

Table
of
Contents

Introduction

This book you are about to read is more than just a book or a guide. It's a journey, a first step toward creating a more understanding, accepting, and awesome world for autistic individuals.

I have dedicated my entire adult life to the research, production of products, and creation of content around autism to foster a more understanding and more educated world. My goal is for autistic individuals like yourself to thrive in a neurotypical world that is often slanted against autistic individuals.

I have set up the world's first neurodiverse panel talks at VidCon (the largest online video conference in the world) and MCM Comic Con.

From briefing the European Parliament on the gap in autistic employment in the world to helping shape the Autism Act for the country of Wales with advisory groups and networking events, I've had opportunities to advocate for myself and others.

This book will take you from where I began right up to the present day, including all the things that I've learned and used to hack life and create a happier existence as an autistic individual. Struggling in school and university, as a partner and a father, in private and in the general public, I needed to try to get by these challenging times.

But I have done more than just get by. I pivoted on those issues and created workarounds, hacks, tools, and tips along the way. I share with you my experiences from this journey.

So please relax, read with an open mind, and try to implement any of the tips and hacks available to you in your life where you feel they could work. I'm not saying everything I suggest in this book is for everybody on the spectrum, but they will work for almost all of us.

Please enjoy this book, as it was a pleasure to write it to share my story, advice, and everything in between with an audience who will really appreciate it and get it. It's not often that we can talk to each other in a way that the quirky oddness of our lives will be understood.

—Daniel M. Jones @TheAspieWorld

Chapter One

Family and Childhood: The Fun and Sad Truth About Autistic Family Life

Being the only autistic member of a family with three siblings wasn't always easy or fun; in fact, I had some super tricky times. However, it was not a negative experience. A lot of the time, I learned things that would really help me later in life.

Anyone can apply these tips, which I gained from my insight and experience over the years. I have laid them out in simple, easy-to-digest takeaway points at the end of each chapter, so that you can instantly start using what I am sharing. It's like I extracted everything functional and rolled it all up into an excellent educational sandwich for you to eat at your leisure . . . and now I'm hungry. But back to my family life . . .

Growing up with a sibling, you see them interacting with other people and with you, and you learn from watching them, even if they steal your favorite toy or are mean for no reason. By being part of a family, you still learn a bunch of stuff to help you survive.

The company Meta has a saying that is almost company policy: "Fail and fail hard." This is because when you fail at something, you learn that the thing that failed was not the path or project for you, so you pivot and move on to something else.

In this chapter, I uncover much of what I learned from family life that helped me as an adult later. By failing, sometimes hard, I can now show you how growing up in an environment that was not autism-friendly actually did me well in the long run. This chapter also covers a lot of insight into feelings and emotions from the dynamic of being "different" in a family unit.

Socializing Challenges

As I mentioned, I come from a family of three children, and both my parents are happily married together to this day. It was interesting for me growing up, and that made it very easy for my struggles to be overlooked. My brother has epilepsy, and my sister is atopic, which means they were both in and out of the hospital all the time. Fun fact: My brother was born with three thumbs!

So here I am, the third born and youngest in my family of three with no obvious health issues. This meant I was, and still am, the most forgotten about in terms of support. Between my brother's epilepsy and my sister's atopy (which often caused asthma and allergic conjunctivitis), my parents were pretty preoccupied.

Given this dynamic, it was often hard to find good examples of socializing behavior. My brother and sister got along and played together well, but they are older than me by several years, so we didn't really get to play all that often together. We would randomly play together, but I needed help understanding the games they wanted to play. I couldn't interact with them in the way they wanted me to because they were talking about stuff that I simply didn't understand.

My brother is a gay man, and he enjoys the company of women, so he had a lot in common with my sister, and they got along well. This left me with not having a traditional male role model in my house because my dad always worked.

My sister was here, there, and everywhere with my brother, so mainly it was just me and my mum, who isn't the most motherly of people.

So how did I handle these socializing challenges? Legos®. Everything was okay because I had Legos. Legos are the most amazing thing, ever my saving grace.

If you will, Legos, to me, were escapism. It was the way I could create a world where I felt safe just by submerging myself in the idea of building something by hand. I loved Legos; I loved making things.

I even transposed from just Legos to building things out of wood and electronics. When I was about eight years old, I adapted some typical kids' army walkie-talkies that my parents had given me for Christmas. I adapted them to work over a longer range so that I could talk to my buddy in his house, who lived about a mile and a half away.

Not only this, I also threw myself into computing. I really, really loved computing technology. I'd surround myself with computers, video games, and other electrical, technical gadgets. My favorite thing was the Commodore 64 and the Nintendo Entertainment System. Like Legos, both gave me an escape from reality to a more basic binary understanding of a world. I could compute because back in the early '90s, everything had to be written in code on a Commodore 64, even word processing.

Sensory Issues

Being the youngest in a family of three, I always had the second round of hand-me-down clothes, shoes, and toys. I didn't mind having hand-me-down toys because I was given a lot of Lego sets from my brother and his friends whose parents were like, "What do we do with all of these Lego bricks?"

I loved having the toys, but I was not too fond of the clothes because of all the jeans. I have, among all the other things in my life, a diagnosis of sensory processing disorder (SPD).

SPD causes me to have an aversion to certain types of material, including that of the rusty, rigid denim of the old-school jeans from the '80s and '90s (YUCK). Most autistic people have sensory issues even if they don't have SPD.

My mother, a self-taught seamstress, used to make clothes, and she was always trying to put me in the clothes she had made. Because we were not the most financially blessed family, we had to make do with hand-me-downs and homemade clothes.

Unfortunately for my mother, I disliked all the clothes she wanted to put me in, especially jeans; they are a big no-no for me.

Jeans made me feel uncomfortable. Wearing them made me feel like I was exposed or violated in some way or awkward to the point that I felt sick to my stomach and just needed to go home and go to bed.

There's a picture of me at my grandparents' 50th wedding anniversary in the early '90s, and I'm wearing jeans. I'm so upset that I'm just flat, and my dad is picking me up to make me feel better. This was a daily occurrence for me, but nobody understood.

My mother would always say, "Come on Dan, stop being so miserable." I was very shy and reserved as these were just ways of coping with the overstimulated sensory environment I was constantly in with my parents.

I guess anybody would think I was a miserable, unhappy, or sad child. I even remember my dad told me once that I was not as happy as my parents wanted me to be.

When was I happy? As long as I wasn't in jeans, I was ecstatic to be at home watching *X-Men* on VHS, playing with my Transformers toys, or making Lego buildings and structures day in and day out.

Sleep Issues

Having an undiagnosed autism spectrum disorder as a kid meant I had a huge issue with sleep. It was almost like I had a sleep aversion, if you will; it wasn't insomnia.

It was more of an inability to fall asleep because of having ADHD (attention-deficit/hyperactivity disorder) and autism. My brain was going two thousand miles an hour.

Every night I tried my best to go to sleep, but I couldn't. So, I just started putting a Star Wars movie on an old VHS black-and-white television somebody had given to my parents. My parents eventually moved the television and VHS player into my room and allowed me to watch movies all I wanted to because they knew that audiovisuals were important to me.

I was in love with Star Wars, and still am. I even wrote a best-selling book called *Become the Force*, inspired by Star Wars. I used to watch Star Wars every day, morning and night, before school and before bed. It was a way to relax and get my stuff set up for the day, get myself aligned with things that I knew were comfortable.

This simple routine made me happy and made me feel somewhat stronger to deal with and cope with the absolute atrocity of the world that I was about to be thrown into by going outside of my comfy domain.

Star Wars helped me cope with people because I used to see Han Solo and Luke Skywalker battling through dozens and dozens of people and getting to the end goal of flying a spaceship or cracking the code to enter the eastern part of a space station. To me, this was a parallel to my life. I had to crack the code, get past the kids, and get into school, so I could eventually get my bag and go home and get back in my space. It was like I was going back to my home planet after spending every day on the Death Star, and it never got any better.

Like the Millennium Falcon, the autistic brain often wonders off into hyperspace to find things to keep us occupied when our bodies just want to sleep. If you can create something that will keep the wondering mind of your autistic brain occupied, it will allow you to actually get some rest.

Benefits of Survival Mode

When you're autistic and growing up with siblings, you feel you have nowhere safe to go to shut the world out. Once my brother moved out and I had my own space, it opened my eyes to feeling relaxed in a room for the first time.

My sister was a social, friendly, bubbly girl, so she used to go out to see all of her friends. After a while, quiet time in my house became the norm because there was a difference in the family dynamic: It was just me at home and my parents when they were not at work. The peace and safety of this setting was almost perfect.

When I was eleven years old, my parents lost their business. They lost their house, and we had to move into social housing. This is quite distressing because when you get used to your environment, it becomes your safe space.

I am a person who is dependent on safe spaces, like a bedroom, a sensory tent in the living room, or even just an area of the house that is quiet and calm. I need this to feel confident and loved.

But all in an instant, everything around me was gone.

I'd lost my house, my bedroom, my safe space in the world. My safety blanket was removed, and I had to enter survival mode when I was moved to a social housing street with some very "interesting" characters.

I think my first experience with the street that we moved to was that our next-door neighbor was a drug dealer, and the police kept raiding his house to arrest him. It was quite shocking for me.

Thinking back to it, I swear I had a lot of trauma within three years of moving out of my old home. I saw the guy next door argue with my father. I also saw lots and lots of drunken fights in the street. I even witnessed a person my age stab themselves and die.

It felt like an uncomfortable, unsafe zone, but I used it as a learning opportunity.

You can do this too. Just give yourself a simple reminder that when you are confronted with something that is potentially worrisome or scary, you can pivot away from these events in the future to safeguard yourself. Knowing that the street was troublesome for me, I learned to stay indoors and only skateboard in safe places, like the park.

Moving to that new street opened my eyes to the world and allowed me to soak in many newfound cultures and adapt somewhat accordingly to the situation. I found myself masking and feeling more in control because, once I realized I could run back to my new home if things were not going well, I had a safe space to practice talking to new people. I was completely new to them, and they didn't know me from Adam, so that was cool.

Regardless, it was difficult to talk to people because I couldn't anticipate their reactions. So why would I bother wasting time if I didn't know what the reaction was going to be?

The first time I spoke to someone who wasn't a friend or family member pushed me right back into survival mode. It happened a few years after I had taught myself music and how to play multiple instruments at the age of fifteen. My favorites to play were the bass and the drums, as these allow you to count and feel the vibrations to predict what happens next— something that autistic people strive to achieve.

After starting a band, I decided to put on a musical event with some other musicians in the local area, and we had to consult with the locals living around the park where the event would take place.

My dad and I met with a local council official and agreed it was okay to do it as long as we went around and spoke to the owners of the houses opposite and adjacent to the area that we would be playing music in. My dad was the primary spokesperson and kept talking to everyone; he was good at it.

When it became my turn to go and speak to someone, I had to walk down the garden path, knock on the door, and talk to them about the event. Before that moment, I was a person who had not spoken to someone outside of the household or friend group.

I was super scared, but I did it. I walked over and knocked on the door, then looked back at my father, thinking I needed his help as I was about to pass out, but he was at the gate, and I was all the way down to the door.

And just then, a person came out. I tried my best to relay the information that my father had said previously to the other residents, but I couldn't get it out properly.

The person was looking confused and starting to get angry at me, so I was about to bail, but my father stepped in and took over that conversation. I gave up then and fled, leaving my father to take over talking to the other houses.

This escape for survival wasn't okay to me. I felt defeated by the fact that I was unable to talk to people, new people and neighbors or just people we encounter in life, and it scared me. I thought, "Hey, I'm never gonna be able to speak to anyone again."

Regardless, the event went ahead, and it was great. It was a good time, and I hit the local news.

Another one of these moments in my life when I completely froze and didn't know what on earth to do was when my parents and their cousins all gathered for an annual Christmas party.

I loved the fact that I got to see my family members at these gatherings, but I absolutely despised the fact that I had to be around drunken people, lots of noise, cigarette smoke, and just general chaos.

During this particular party, I remember I was so tired that I fell asleep, and one of my parents picked me up and put me to sleep in my cousin's bed because she was at her university. The next morning, I woke up completely disoriented. I didn't know where I was, and I was utterly alone in my cousin's house. I just froze. I didn't talk to my family members who lived there, and I wouldn't eat. I couldn't do anything. I just had to wait until my parents came to pick me up, but they were hungover. I wish they'd never done that because, to me, it was a breaking of trust. I felt like I couldn't trust my parents to keep me safe anymore, which is a big deal for somebody on the spectrum, especially when that somebody is also a child of maybe seven years old.

However traumatic these events were, I realized I was being put into situations that pushed me into lockdown for survival. And often, it would be situations I would never be in if I had a diagnosis when I was three or four. Most of the situations happened because my parents were treating me as a typical child, and exposing me to typical things.

The downside was, of course, I was sad, scared, and alone a lot of the time. The benefit is that this exposure was actually giving me data to process on how to deal with people. It was a kind of shock therapy for uncomfortable situations that made me realize I survived.

Trust in Yourself Leads to Confidence

Trust and validation are two main areas in which we, as autistic people, need to feel safe. If you have no trust, then you won't feel safe, and if you have no validation, you have little to no self-confidence.

My parents never made me feel as though they had my back; I wanted more reassurance and trust.

I remember my mum had signed me up for some kind of national statistics program where I had to be interviewed by the government every four or five years about my interests, fears, and personality.

I didn't like it. A stranger talking to me about things that I wouldn't want to talk to anyone about? How could she not know this would be upsetting?

By the time I was about ten, I knew I didn't want to do it again. So, I asked my mother to cancel it and not to allow them back.

I got in from school one day, and the government was there again to do the survey.

I couldn't believe it! My mother had either forgotten to tell them to not come, or she was ignoring my needs. I freaked out and told her I don't ever want do that again. She apologized and said we wouldn't do it again.

Four years later . . . yup, you guessed it! Another guy knocked on the door to interview me.

At this point, I'd had enough, and I was old enough to say no. But the damage was done. My trust had been repeatedly betrayed. In my mind, my parents could never be trusted to keep me safe, which is an unfortunate harsh reality.

Loss of trust was only one side to this experience though. The flip side is that I learned that if I want to get ahead in life as an autistic person, I need a voice, a voice that I control, a voice that has volume and can take a stance because I am in control of myself.

You can build trust in yourself to create confidence by using small daily mantras or rituals. If you tell yourself in the morning that today is going to be a good day, and you can trust in yourself, this builds instant confidence. Doing this along with the superman pose with your arms on your hips and your chest out adds a huge confidence boost. Although this may seem odd or silly, the more you do this, the easier it feels. As practice makes progress, you'll be a superhero in no time.

One thing I try to say to myself daily is "Every day and in every way, I am getting better." This was how I started to build confidence and self-worth, because I had validation and trust in myself to get things done.

Actionable Takeaway Points

- Overcome socializing challenges by observing those who are good at socializing, and by taking breaks for "escapism."

- Balance overstimulation with quiet, reserved time. This could be sitting in a quiet room reading, or having two minutes alone in your garden away from the environment you were just in. It is about interrupting the cycle of overstimulation.

- Battle sleep issues by finding a mental focus (mine was audiovisual).

- Remember that survival mode is like shock therapy (learning new ways to deal with people). Trusting and validating yourself creates confidence and develops your own voice.

Chapter Two

Friendship and You: How You Can Make Friends Even If You Think You Can't

There is a massive misconception that autistic people cannot make friends.

I mean, this couldn't be more wrong. It is not that, as autistic people, we cannot make friends; our difficulty lies in *finding* friends.

I can 100 percent say that you have had at least one friend in your life so far, and this is living proof that a lot of what people say about us is, in fact, not actually applicable. Even if you haven't had that one friend, the ability you possess to love your favorite topics illustrates that you can care deeply and connect with others.

There are many reasons for this confusion, most stemming from the difficulty we have in seeking out people who can understand us on our level and who we can understand on their level.

I have a pool of friends. It wasn't always like this, and it isn't always easy, but it is doable and 100 percent achievable for all autistic people.

This chapter is dedicated to autistic people finding friends and keeping friends. I cover the ins and outs of all the friendships I have had and how I manage to find and make loyal friends. You can use all the tips in this chapter to create long-lasting relationships in your life.

Find Common Ground

Okay, so we've all been there for that moment of self-awesomeness when you want to make friends and you think to yourself, "Heck yeah, I got this! I can totally go over there and start talking to these cool people and make friends . . ." Then you actually do go over there, but you stop suddenly and start looking at the people. They look back at you, and then the fear of actually talking runs through your body, instantly making you feel like you are having one of those dreams where you are trying to speak but your mouth won't work. On top of it all, you are a sweaty anxious mess . . . What? Just me?

I know it's not just me, as there are many awesome autistic individuals who want to brave it all and make some friends, perhaps creating new friends to add to our already existing coven of nerds, but the harsh reality of this is that we all find it difficult.

I also feel that it doesn't get any easier as we grow older. Trying to make friends in my thirties is just as tricky as it was in my teens.

At about six or seven years old, I remember being at school and trying to talk to other kids. When I went over, I didn't know what words to use, so I ended up just staring at them very creepily like some weird-ass Halloween doll from a horror movie or something!

This, of course, didn't go well. They ended up getting too freaked out and didn't want to play with me, so we didn't end up being friends.

However, I found some progress at this time with a different approach, which leads me to one of the hacks I use to find and make friends to this day. My first experience with it led to making friends with someone who I am still excellent friends with to this day.

Back in the late '80s and early '90s, I was a huge fan of Weebles. Yes, we all know they wobble but don't fall down (I knew you'd be saying this in your head, if you're old enough to remember the advertisement that is). At school, there was a Weebles airplane in a lovely maroon color that was like a kid magnet. It was so shiny and bubble shaped; it was just amazing!

At the time I spotted this plane, it was currently in the hands of a skilled toy operator named Lee Williams. As I approached him with awe in my eyes over this airplane, Lee turned while playing with the toy. Looking at me through his '80s bowl haircut, he smiled and passed me the plane!

Wow, I thought with surprise, that was super easy, but why and how? Okay, so I have many questions . . .

Now about this time in your journey through this book, you are totally sitting there just nodding your head like, THIS IS ME! Yes! You are autistic, you are amazing, and this is totally you! Okay, back to the story.

I was so shocked that this kid, who wasn't obliged to play with or be kind to me, was able to do both out of his own free will, without my creepy stalker pose. How did this happen? Then it clicked! Ah ha! Just like Einstein jumping out of the bath saying eureka, I figured it out!

Lee wanted to play with me and share toys because we both liked the same toys; we both were big fans of the Weebles.

Okay, okay, I know what you are thinking: "So Dan, what do the Weebles have to do with friendship?" It is very simple. Lee and I had common ground, which is the starting basis for any relationship. If you are starting a romantic relationship or a friendship with someone, you have to have something in common to be able to relate to one another.

Why is this? Well, common interest creates communication possibilities. For example, a person who is interested in *World of Warcraft* will know a lot about the game, and if they come across another person who is really into *World of Warcraft*, then they will both be interested in knowing what the other person has to say on this topic.

Make Connections Through Your Current Friends

Once you've found your common ground and made a new friend, you can branch out through your friend. In high school, Lee introduced me to Warhammer model painting and took me to a lunchtime in-school club where I saw other enthusiastic teens eager to paint their latest dragon or troll miniature figurine.

This was awesome! Not only was I able to do something I enjoyed in school, but also Lee introduced me to other people who I then became friends with.

All of the anxiety of wondering how I needed to act or what I needed to say to be able to make friends with these people disappeared. I already knew I had lots of things to talk to them about and ask them questions about because they shared a common interest and friend with me. This combination was the perfect formula for making friends, and I have used it ever since.

I was also able to use these friendship hacks to become lifelong friends with Jake Jones-Williams. He and I are now in a band together called Straight Jacket Legends and have released records in the U.K., Japan, and the United States. But music is not how we met.

I only got to know Jake because I found out he was asking around in school if anyone was interested in buying or selling vintage Star Wars action figures. As an avid Star Wars fan myself, and also a HUGE vintage Star Wars figure collector, I was destined to meet him. Thankfully, a friend told me about Jake. We met up and exchanged action figures. From there, Jake introduced me to music. As I am a multi-instrumentalist, we started a band, which meant connecting to even more friends.

None of the experiences I have had making friends were filled with intense amounts of effort. In fact, it was minimal, and often unplanned, effort. The common interests created the initial connection, and the personality of the persons involved continued the friendship.

I hear all the time that autistic people can't make friends; I even hear it from our own community of autistic individuals. This makes me sad because I know how amazing every autistic person I have ever met is and how much they have to give to a community that accepts and loves them. I just wish they had the confidence to find the circles, groups, and events they are into and actually attend.

This is one of the main driving forces for this chapter. YES, I am talking to YOU! You are amazing and can make the best of friends with someone, I just know it. Believe in yourself and see what happens.

To this day, when parents ask me for advice for their kids to make more friends or create social relationships, I always start with this question: What are they interested in? Once I know this, I tell the parents to check out after-school clubs, in-school clubs, Facebook groups, live events, and conventions or conferences and take them to these things. I actively promote this method as the main way to make friends for autistic individuals and always put this advice in my live speaking events when I am doing a keynote or a presentation.

Actionable Takeaway Points

- Find common ground through your interests.

- Look for local groups, clubs and events that are in your topic of interest. This can be done with a simple Google search.

- Look up online groups on forums and Facebook for like-minded individuals. You will find a ton of groups, so just read the descriptions and see which ones relate to you.

- Connect with friends of your friends by hanging out together, as you probably all have similar interests.

- Always believe in yourself that you are able to make connections with people. A self-confirming idea that you can and you will make friends is a confidence boost that will pay off.

- Collect Star Wars action figures. (Just joking!)

Chapter Three

Dating on the Spectrum: Can Autistic People Fall in Love?

It's so interesting to think that people have actually asked me if autistic people can fall in love or even have sex.

It is pretty remarkable. However, there are more complex answers to all of the questions people have about autism and relationships.

I have been in relationships since high school, and it has been super challenging at times. I am raw, honest, and to the point in this chapter so you can understand more about the successful side of relationships that I have had. The points I outline in this chapter can be used to strengthen a relationship and create a better bond with your loved one.

The problem is that people are never 100 percent honest about this subject because of embarrassment or because it's too taboo.

That is, until now.

"Can you have sex?"

Oh man, that question. You know, oddly enough, this is a question I get asked so many times, and it's always unreal to me that someone asks this. But they do . . . often.

People seem to think that just because you are on the autism spectrum, you are some intellectually inept recluse that is devoid of any human emotion or interaction, including romantic relationships and physical touch. This is only partly true! Just kidding . . . kind of . . .

So let me start at the beginning, just so you can follow along at the same speed I am.

Environmental Sensitivities

As autistic people, we are highly sensitive to sensory stimuli (hypersensitivity); this means we can have a heightened, oversensitivity to stimulation from things like noise, smell, touch, or temperature. You know when you have difficulty sitting in a busy café, or riding a public bus, or even shopping next to the deli counter because of the smells coming off the highly flavored food (like their freshly chopped raw onion and garlic)? It's that mix of sensory input.

However, in the same breath, there are some of us who are under sensitive (hyposensitivity) to the same input of sensory stimuli. This means that we may be unaware of people calling our names, or not realize we are overheating when we are wearing huge coats in the middle of summer in high heat.

I have to also add here (and I'm honestly not trying to confuse you), there are some of us who experience a mix of both hyper- and hyposensitivity. What do I mean? So, you could have an autistic person who feels oversensitive to a light touch from another person, but is under sensitive to sound and may really enjoy loud music.

Okay, now that the background stuff is out of the way, let's get to the juicy part!

So, sex . . . do autistic people have sex?

In the simple and short way of answering: Yes, of course we do! But let's be clear on this; it isn't a simple yes. It's not a "Yes, of course, just like anyone else does" guarantee.

There are more interesting insights into this than a surface answer of simply saying yes. The truth of this is that we, as autistic people, are so varied as individuals and there are many different needs that have to be met in certain situations to make each of us open to comfort and intimacy.

Let me give you a metaphor. (*By the way, I'm learning more about how to understand metaphors, which can be difficult for autistic people. Hands up if you are here, but I enjoy making them so buckle up!*)

Let's say a person is in the middle of a busy train station. It is midday, and people are coming on and off the train. It's fast, noisy, very busy, and crowded with people. Imagine someone asking a random person, "Would you have sex here with your partner?" Their simple answer might be, "Yes, I love my partner and would make love anywhere." But, this setting isn't exactly romantic or private and, let's face it, you are going to end up in jail for the night if you try.

Now, that was an extreme example, I get that. But the autistic mind is living in the extreme every day. There are so many variables that impact the sensory environment that we exist in, and these variables can cause many different outcomes. Have you ever done that thing that really pisses your parents off? Let's say you really enjoy spaghetti in a restaurant but if your mum made that meal at home, you wouldn't eat it and you'd be put off by it? Or think about how you really enjoy watching movies at home but wouldn't go to the movies to see a big screen movie.

It's all about your environment and how the sensory input is impacting your ability to be in that moment comfortably.

For Intimacy, Communication is Key

So, let's get back to intimacy! Touch can be tricky to navigate. Some of us may like hugs, but only soft hugs or hard hugs. For me, it's the latter: I can only enjoy a hug if it is a firm pressure-based hug. That being said, let's not forget that there are some of us who may not like hugging at all. For intimacy to happen, touch preferences and sensitivities need to be known.

For example, there is something funny that happens between me and my partner when we are driving in our car. We would be driving along, and my partner (bless her) would put her hand softly on my leg in an attempt to be affectionate and supportive, as any loving partner would do. The funny part is, as soon as she touches me lightly on my leg, I literally jump out of my seat with a bit of a surprised screech and a dash of panic! Then she apologizes, I calm down, and we both laugh about it.

In all honesty, her light touch on my leg is like an electric shock-wave pulsing through my entire body with a sharp current that hits me, like jumping into an ice-cold lake in the middle of winter with no wetsuit on. (I see you smiling to yourself, many of us get this feeling.) This may sound extreme to non-autistic people, like: "Dan, your missus just touched your leg, what the heck?" But this is truly what it is like. I cannot control it or help it, that is just the way my brain is wired for this type of sensory input.

So, as you can imagine, this does require some interesting rules when getting intimate, whether it be cuddling, receiving or giving hugs, or more. The rules become even more complex when you both have different preferences or triggers. If you want to hug someone, they also have to understand and want the same pressure as you when hugging, be it light or hard, to make this a successful transaction.

There are many things you may experience that are highly personal and individual to your needs when it comes to feeling comfortable and ready for intimacy, so take the time to self-assess and determine what rules you'll need.

There is one last issue that I find comes up a lot, and it is a pretty big one. It is good to note that at some point, we may reject a request for intimacy due to nothing else but the environment (remember the train station metaphor?). The issue is that a non-autistic partner may feel rejected, and that sense of rejection could create tension and issues in the relationship if sensitivities are not discussed or understood in advance.

Actionable Takeaway Points

- Make sure that you express your wants and needs clearly to your partner to get the best flow of communication with them.

- Listen to yourself; get to know your needs and likes.

- Remember that sensory input from the environment can impact your mood, so do not think you are wrong in how you feel, just make sure to explain this to your partner.

Chapter Four

School Life: What You Need to Know to Hack Academia

In my life, I attended primary school, which is elementary or junior high school for anyone who is American (I see you). I've also attended high school, three courses at technical college, and a university where I got my BSc in chemistry. I have had my fair share of academic experience.

But what was that like as an autistic individual? Did I enjoy it? Did I succeed? Did I fail?

Well, since I do have that degree in chemistry, I didn't fail overall; however, I didn't complete any academia in the typical sense. I had to work harder, figure out new ways of doing things, and find workarounds for my autism that I had to use; otherwise, I would have failed.

In fact, many autistic people fail at the college level. This is down to a few causes, like a lack of appropriate support and mentorship, co-occurring mental health issues, and a lack of reasonable adjustments.

For autistic people like us, just failing at school could add to our mental health issues and cause many bigger problems.

Overcoming all of these obstacles caused an overwhelming feeling of success once I completed my courses. Luckily for you, I share all of my hacks and workarounds in this chapter, so you'll never miss a beat at academia again!

Educational Challenges for Autistic Learners

School life was . . . How can I put it? I despised primary school and high school. I guess I didn't dislike high school as much because I got to skateboard, play music, and hang out with people who were interested in the same things as me, but for the most part, school sucked big time.

Why did school suck, you ask? I guess it is simple. If you are an undiagnosed autistic person attending school, you become squashed into a box with kids you do not know and cannot talk to. This made it difficult for me.

Not only is it difficult because it's hard to understand what the kids are doing and why they are doing it, but it's also so, so hard to get used to the workload and everything that you have to do academically. This is a major trigger for burnout.

In general, there is a big difference between people's learning types, especially when you attend large schools with lots and lots of children. Being undiagnosed means your learning needs are not easily recognized or addressed. I was unfortunate to be undiagnosed in the '90s while attending primary and high school. This means from the age of three, I attended a school that felt like hell from the moment my parents dropped me off in the morning until I got home.

I'd be so anxious and worried about going in, I wouldn't be able to enjoy my breakfast or enjoy cartoons before school. When I got to school, it was cold sweat time all day, so much so that I was never really that hungry in school because I was so nervous about going there. It was scary and unfamiliar with the smell of the cleaning sanitizing liquid.

The cleaners used on the tables left awful white, powdery residue on your clothes if you leaned on the desk. The chairs that have plastic nibs on each foot grind on that horrible sandpaper-like textured floor and make a noise that is uncomfortable to stomach at the best of times, let alone if you are in a place you already didn't feel comfortable or want to be in.

But like anything else, I stumbled along, trying my best with what I had, which was a moral obligation to try my best and satisfy the thirst to learn.

I enjoyed things like Bible stories because they taught life parables through philosophy. I also enjoyed the science aspect of learning about the mysteries of the world, the universe, and everything in between. However, on many occasions, my parents would be pulled into the school to talk to them about how I'd been too forward in the class because I'd be checking teachers on their inability to teach science correctly.

It was fun to educate teachers because my brother is an intellectual. Since he is quite a few years older than me, he would share a lot of the cool stuff he read in mysticism books or scientific books. I was able to just sit there in awe and wonder as he told me all that new information.

We spent hours looking through science books and geography books and weird phenomena, and I used the knowledge so much in school. Still, eventually this wore off because the teachers weren't impressed, especially when I asked them when I was only five how Mary was able to have a baby if she was a virgin. This didn't sit well with the governing body at school, so they pulled my parents in to talk once again. Hey ho, that's how things go.

Even with the things I enjoyed, school honestly felt like I was being stripped naked, thrown into the street, covered in ice water, and told I had to recite the alphabet backwards. I was alone and trapped somewhere that felt like jail for the longest amount of time. Six hours is an incredible amount of time for a young person who's dealing with crippling anxiety outside of their comfort zone and fear of the world around them.

Through this stress though, it opened me up to what was really going on with my learning type. I figured I could go to school, collect the subject matters, and then go home and research in a way that was easier and more fun for me to digest. I could learn where I could focus while stimming, moving my leg rapidly or standing up, all the things that were not allowed in school.

To this day, I apply this very same principle to everything I learn. I understand the name and genre of the topic I want to know, then independently research it. I did this same thing while attending university for my degree in chemistry.

It wasn't easy to understand what the lecturers were saying to me when I was sitting in the theatre. When they had an accent, I was just floored. There was no way I was retaining anything from them. So, I would make a list of all the topics, then collect all the online data from the university portal. You'd find me sitting in my office until late into the night, teaching myself the information.

Our autistic brains work in a way where we can obtain information and move with it academically, but we each must find the best way to retain and learn the data.

Eliminate or Minimize Known Triggers

One silver lining that came out of my early education days was learning how to recognize and manage my triggers.

I remember every year we did a school play for Christmas. Usually, it would be a typical nativity with Jesus, Mary, the wise men, and all that good stuff.

However, sometimes they would do different plays, like the *Pied Piper of Hamelin* or *Robin Hood*. I was always cast in the play because the school equality rules required including all children.

Unfortunately for me, going up on stage in the front of somebody to say lines was never my cup of tea, so I would always have a walk-on role where I'd be a jester, a juggler, or just somebody in the background. Knowing that I could have a choice and be listened to at the minor level was pretty groundbreaking. Knowing I wouldn't have to go in and be embarrassed, nervous, scared, and anxious for one day helped me recognize and eliminate one of my triggers.

The school plays created a situation that encouraged me to have a voice in education; I could no longer survive by just being mute. The fact that the school plays forced me into a position of self-power (giving me my own actual choice of what I wanted to do) and that I articulated what I wanted filled me with a new confidence. The confidence to be able to verbally say what I wanted to say in situations like this through the rest of my school experience.

I realized that confidence came from the fact I could use my voice to say, "I don't want to" and be acknowledged. This was especially important when having to do things in high school, like group work or reading out loud to the class. By voicing my concerns and talking to the teachers, I was able to avoid this type of situation.

Speaking up and finding ways to compromise with the rules helped manage my triggers. I was constantly being told that I had to wear a specific type of school uniform, which triggered my sensory processing disorder. I managed to minimize that reaction by wearing a different one, but it still had to include a shirt and tie. I am not a shirt-and-tie person. The uniform was still not working well with my sensory issues, so I suggested leaving my tie open at the collar and removing the jumper. I used these little adjustments to survive, so it wasn't constant doom and gloom.

Now let us fast forward to the end of my living hell, aka "primary school." I eventually got to high school in 1997. High school was a massive transition. Not only did I have to learn now how to make friends, I also had to learn how to walk from my house to school.

This was exceptionally difficult for the entire first year of high school because I would get lost trying to go from my house to school. For the first month or two, my sister walked with me, as she was in high school with me for a cross-over period of about two months. But after she left school, I was alone for the longest, scariest walk I had ever endured up to that point.

But right then, at my most terrifying moment of schooling, a miracle in disguise happened. My parents lost their business. It was a coal merchant business where my father would deliver coal to houses all over our county. This kind of industry had a finite life and many obstacles that led to its closure.

The loss of the business wasn't the miracle though. Not even the fact that we lost our family home. The miracle was that the social housing my family and I were placed into was back-to-back with my high school. All I had to do was walk about 10 feet, and I was on the school grounds.

Because the fear of walking to school was eliminated from my life, I could edge myself into going outside my comfort zone, just a little bit. Without the constant worry about walking to and from school each day, I could focus energy on things like trying to make friends or trying to focus more during class.

It was eye-opening for me to realize just how much free mental head space I had to try other things when a significant trigger gets eliminated from my day.

Eliminating known triggers, or using workarounds to soften them, will increase your capacity to focus on other things. In high school, for example, I remember being a loner. I sat alone, ate my packed lunch in the courtyard, and did my best to avoid other students and the loud noise of the bells. Instead of being overwhelmed by my known triggers, I could focus on enjoying my meal or making connections with the friends who understood me. I was able to discover music and teach myself to play instruments because I met people who played music who were really interested in having me in the group.

A friend group is something I never had in primary school because it was such a small school and all the kids wanted to play was football. They most definitely were not into robots, VR, and science like I was.

I decided to focus all my energy in school on something that was creatively fun, so I persevered with classes by managing my triggers so that at lunchtime, I could do what I enjoyed, whether that meant a quiet meal in the courtyard or running home for the period. At home, I could listen to some music, learn how to play bass, guitar, and drums, then run back to school for the rest of my classes before coming straight back home to more music.

Use the Sandwich Method to Manage Triggers You Cannot Control

There was no support for undiagnosed autistic people in my high school. There was no support for autistic people because in 1997 in Anglesey, there was no diagnosis of autism to be given at school age, so they didn't know how to deal with autism. This meant there were a lot of things outside of my control that made school life challenging.

As I said before, I despised school. By high school, I was happiest before school or after. Literally from 3:30 p.m. until 10 p.m., I'd hammer the bass guitar, the six-string electric guitar, acoustic guitar, and the drums every single day. Through this process, I realized I had been managing the uncontrollable (the requirement to go to school) with the sandwich method! It is something I teach in lots of my courses and coaching now. The premise is simple: Sandwich a bad experience that you cannot control between two good experiences that you can control.

This process creates a pattern in your mind that you know you can relax before and after the part of your day you cannot control. For school, this meant about 80 percent of my time I enjoyed, so I could handle the remaining 20 percent of time spent in school.

One time in primary school, I felt so disorientated when the school headmaster changed. I spent three years getting used to one headmaster, and then they switched out overnight for a new one, who stayed for the rest of the time I was there.

I remember feeling like, oh my goodness, now I have nobody to go to with my problems because the headmaster was like the Dean of the School. They listened and understood you. Having that steady presence suddenly vanish was jarring, but at the same time, it was one of my sink-or-swim moments.

You will have many sink-or-swim moments in your life. You can keep swimming so long as you hold on to your self-confidence (which we've been building by speaking up for ourselves to eliminate triggers) and the positive experiences you look forward to each day (the bread of your sandwich). You will never sink as long as you know you have something to work toward. Remember that everything we do is simply a way to figure out what works. If you feel like you are failing at something, just know that it was a test that proves that way wasn't the right way for you and it's time to use another way.

Another trigger that was beyond my control was surviving special education. My parents tried somewhat to get me extra help. They had me attend the special education unit in the primary school, which wasn't very good. It was a section in the library of the school where a special teacher came and taught me how to read, write, and talk to people, but it didn't do any good because of the environment. I didn't enjoy being lumped in with the naughty kids and struggled to focus through those circumstances. It was a very isolating experience from the ages of three to eleven; I had never felt so alone while surrounded by so many people. Focusing on getting home to the comfort and safety of my room and my favorite activities helped me work through it.

You know what else was awful and beyond my control? Primary school sports days or gym events; those were the worst. I'm not too fond of sports; I didn't like getting sweaty and running around because your clothes get sweaty and sticky, which is a sensory overload trigger. I never use the word "hate" because it's not a good word to use; however, in this situation, I can definitely say I hated sports day. It was always in the summer, and the sun was so harsh on my eyes and my skin. I just couldn't deal with being outside running around in the sun. This is just another example of the school's lack of accommodation for children on the autism spectrum with sensory triggers. I always tried to use an excuse to get out of gym days (eliminating the trigger), but often I had to participate.

My parents knew that these days were too overloading for me, so after a sports day event, they would take me home immediately and get something like a Ribena juice box, put on *Sesame Street*, and allow me to decompress because I needed to relax after it. Knowing I had this part of the "sandwich" to look forward to helped me hang in there when I could not get out of gym.

The actual academic side of school was difficult too. By high school, the teachers were more in tune with true academia and facts, so I didn't have to worry about them saying the wrong thing. However, they were not accommodating of my ADHD or my struggle with the auditory learning style. They continued to provide verbal instruction from the front of the class even when it was clear I could not understand or learn this way. Having to face this struggle every day and push myself to work harder to learn in a way that made sense to me was balanced only by the safety and enjoyment I knew I would feel back at home.

Use School Clubs and Resources to Grow Socially and Academically

In school you are a lone wolf. You still have to survive; no one can do your work for you. Nobody can make friends for you, and nobody can be you. Only you can be you. But that doesn't mean you can't put yourself out there to meet others or get help when you need it.

For autistic individuals, this is very hard because making friends or speaking up for yourself isn't easy. Like I mentioned before, a friend introduced me to my first club in high school. It was something that interested me right off the bat. It was called the Warhammer Painting Club, where you buy these Warhammer models, small figures like Dungeons & Dragons™ characters, and you paint them and decorate them.

This was a lunchtime activity that killed two birds with one stone for me. I was able to find like-minded people with whom I could build potential camaraderie and friendship with so I wouldn't feel so alone. This also allowed me to do something during lunchtime rather than just freak out and eat my lunch alone.

This can be something that you can do in your own situation. Pick a topic that you are super into and find clubs and activities around your interest. Once you do this, you will be able to find other people like you who are into the same things. That will allow you to branch out and make new friends.

This is how most of high school went for me, but the real test of academia came when I was in college and university. Here in the U.K., technical college happens between the ages of 16 and, say, 20, when you attend an introductory course to set you up for the course that you want to do in university on a degree level.

I was initially involved in performing arts and music; it was terrific. I got to express myself musically—I also did a fair amount of acting, dancing, and singing. It was great! I had really good people around me, and it was probably one of the best years of my life.

Unfortunately, though, because I was hyperactive and still an undiagnosed autistic, I needed help and support. Even though I was seeing the school's counselor and the mental health team, I was asked to bring a report card to class every day so that teachers could monitor my behavior and sign off if I behaved. I was hyperactive and disruptive in class, but a report card isn't usually something you have in more mature academic settings like a technical college or university. When it happened to me, I was so distraught and destroyed by the whole experience. If I had gotten more academic support, I might have avoided this. But I learned that hack in university.

I got a degree at university in chemistry, which is quite a disciplined degree that I love because of mathematics and complex ideas about the universe and all the juicy things. However, I had no idea how to organize my work, manage my time, read all of my books with dyslexia, and everything else in between.

It was around this time that I had a dyslexia test done, and I was also diagnosed with autism and ADHD. This made me aware of the resources available that could help me with those academic challenges I faced.

The university's School of Chemistry offered and implemented a note taker for me that was to come to the lectures to take notes for me and a lab hand who could help me in my labs and would also help me organize my lab work. They also provided a student mentor who I could go and see every week to discuss problems, issues, and everything that concerned me.

This was fantastic, as they helped me organize all of my paperwork and notes in an excellent way. I can't stress enough the importance of asking for help. Find out what resources your school or university offers and take advantage.

Now, thanks to those resources, the following are the best tips for hacking academia that I took away from my experiences.

- **Collect all paper handouts and number and date the pages.** Got teachers that come in and give you handout after handout? Each week you end up with a stack of handouts that have no formal organization and it's overwhelming. So, as soon as you get a handout, write the page number and date at the top of it. You then repeat this process with an increment of pages for that day. Then you repeat the process for consecutive days, changing the date as you go. You'll end up with a complete and utterly comprehensive list of date-organized and page-numbered handouts. You could even group together and staple the papers to keep in a plastic wallet for review time.

- **Collect all the key points of learning items, then do solo research so you can understand at your own pace and learning type.** Have a syllabus or key term list for your course? Outside of class, look up the information at your own pace using your own methods. This way you'll be using your own learning style to master the material.

- **Use a smartphone or tablet to record audio lectures and take pictures of essential slides.** Every day I went to lectures, I would get so distracted by silly things like flies in the room, lights, or even a red pen just sitting there. Suddenly, I'd realize I just blanked out for 50 percent of the lecture. Setting up your phone or iPad to record the audio of the lecture allows you to listen again, repeating parts of the speech that you miss or find difficult and transposing the information into the written word. If there are slides but no slide handouts, use your phone to take a picture of the slide and turn it into a PDF document that you can print out and keep with the notes from that day.

Whether you get help from the student support system or use your own tools (iPhone, iPad), find the methods that work best for you to get the most out of areas in study that you find challenging.

Actionable Takeaway Points

- Identify your educational challenges and triggers, then find ways to eliminate or minimize them.
- Use the sandwich method to overcome daily uncomfortable times or triggers you cannot control or avoid.
- Join school clubs and identify available school resources you could use.

- Collect all paper handouts, then number and date the pages.

- Figure out the key learning topics, then do some solo research to understand at your own pace with your own learning style. Use a smartphone or tablet to record audio lectures and take pictures of essential slides.

- Use a smartphone or tablet to record audio lectures and take photos of essential slides. You can then turn these photos into PDFs for future reference.

- Use the audio recordings to create Word documents.

Chapter Five

Before Your Diagnosis: What I Learned at School and How You Can Avoid the Same Issues Being Undiagnosed

---

This chapter discusses my thoughts, feelings, and understanding of the world as I was growing up and navigating through schooling before I was diagnosed autistic. By sharing my experience, I know that you will be able to smile and nod along, as you probably have shared these same experiences as me.

The world of an undiagnosed autistic person can be terrifying and overwhelming; however, there are many things that I learned from these experiences that, although uncomfortable, I can use and have used to my advantage.

This chapter will help change the way you think of negative situations growing up and open your mind to the potential that was always there, but you didn't see it at the time because you were overwhelmed.

Let's start at the beginning, the '90s. What can I say? Oh boy, here we go. Way back in 1997 (when I started high school)—no wait! I'll get to that a little later; let's start way back at the beginning!

Okay, so picture this. It's 1989, and we all had questionable haircuts, but we also had the best toys and cartoons; we can't have it all.

Wow, this is it; this is where we all start our journey in life, from careers to friends. It's all down to this pinnacle moment, and as I know, first impressions are everything. Or so my parents had me believe. They told me that this was the most important moment of my life and everything starts here: primary school.

It sucked!

I was three years old and about to embark on my education pathway for the first time. I started attending primary school in the small Welsh town of Holyhead, where I lived and still live to this day. I attended the Parc School Nursery classes, which were on from 9 a.m. until 11 a.m. every weekday.

A typical morning would usually see me hoping to God that I was going to come down with the flu, a cold, or something that would justify my inability to go to school that day. I used to pray and pray that I'd wake up and school would be cancelled, or there be a snowstorm, or just randomly the school would say it's closed because every single day felt like I was being stripped naked and thrown into the street in the middle of winter: raw and exposed.

First off, I found it super difficult to go to school because of the three-block journey outdoors, which to me felt like that scene in the movie *Beetlejuice*, when the newly deceased main characters open the front door to the house to try and go outside and a sand monster tries to eat them. The whole world is scary, so they're only safe inside their house. This is how I explain what my childhood felt like when going from my house to school, even though it was only a short distance away.

Being in school, I had to not only try to understand what the other kids were saying to other classmates and to me, but I also had to try to understand what on earth each of the teachers was asking of me. It's kind of like when you haven't been updated on the fact that your extended family is coming over for holiday dinner and you are trying to battle with dealing with the input of everything and everyone, which is difficult for us autistics.

I had to try and seem interested in the most mundane, boring, and (at times) incorrect information the teachers were giving us on science and nature. Every single second felt like an hour.

I felt so uncomfortable, I despised wearing school uniforms, and all I really wanted to do was go home in the sanctuary of my bedroom and learn about VR, robots, and rockets. But no, I had to stay and endure this awful place. At least, that's how it felt for me in my mind; I'm sure the school was good for other kids, as both my brother and sister happily attended this very same school.

Communication, Learning, and Socializing Challenges

COMMUNICATION

Autistic people sometimes struggle with communication, as they are often too direct. For example, when I was in school, a teacher was trying to teach us about speed. She tried to explain the difference between the speed of light and the speed of sound. Now, it's common knowledge that the speed of light is faster than the speed of sound because we have planes that can break the sound barrier but not the light barrier. On this particular day in this particular lesson, however, the teacher tried to explain to us the difference using thunderstorms.

She stated that in a thunderstorm, you hear the thunder and then see the lightning, so sound travels faster than light. It was at this moment I facepalmed and had to say something. In my "too direct" way of communicating, I shouted out that she was wrong! The teacher looked at me and asked why. I then began to explain the airplane example and also just the fact that the speed of light is unobtainable by today's propulsion methods. She downplayed my contribution and said, "Oh well, I'll check later and see if you are right, but I'll carry on with this for now."

Her blatant dismissal of my data was likely because she was unsure of the information, intimidated by my level of intellect at that age, or embarrassed about our exchange in front of the entire class. Whatever the reason, my attempt at communicating failed and what's worse is the fact that she continued to teach the wrong data to the kids. I think I really fell out of love with school for good at this point in life.

LEARNING

Autistic learners often struggle to figure out their preferred learning styles. When I was young, even knowing my interests and learning style only helped so long as the school let me explore them. For example, I really enjoyed computers; actually, I was pretty much obsessed with this old-school version of Wikipedia we had in the '90s called Encarta. Now, if you remember this, congratulations! You are as old as or older than me, and your back hurts.

Encarta used a compact disc that you'd have to buy every year to keep the information up to date. Highly inefficient, but that was the only way to keep up with the data.

In my primary school, I would be allowed to sit every break time or indoor playtime and read, learn, and explore the world of computing. This involved me obsessively staring at information and pictures on virtual reality, robotics, engineering, electronics, chemistry, and more. You name it, I was looking at it on Encarta.

But the school didn't always get this right. Sometimes, they would just force me to go outside, which was completely out of my comfort zone and outside of my ability to function as a normal human being (yes, I'm that dramatic, but also you know exactly what I mean).

SOCIALIZING

I remember precisely one time that I was outside, alone as usual, because my friends could talk to other kids and they got along, but I could only talk to friends about Star Wars or robots or the Hulk or something ridiculous that nobody else wanted to talk about. On this particular day, I thought to myself, "I know a joke that I could use to break the ice and make other kids laugh." It was *Beetlejuice* again that I got this from, and yes, it sounds like my parents had no problem with keeping me from watching things that weren't appropriate for my age (*sarcasm here, by the way . . . just wanted to point that out, since we autistics need help to recognize that sometimes*).

Anyway, the specific joke I told was something about the part of the movie when the character Beetlejuice kind of spits in his coat and says, "I'm gonna save it for later."

Now, the reaction of my family was that everyone laughed at this part of the film, so me being me, I figured it could work in school. Also, I had no idea what was funny about that scene (*shocker, I didn't get the joke*), but I figured if I used this as a way to kind of break the ice, maybe the kids would think I'm funny and I'd be able to make friends and get along.

This didn't happen. In actual fact, the kids thought what I was doing was stupid and just continued to ignore me. That's okay. I didn't mind being the odd kid. I didn't want to be forced to try and be "normal" anyway. But this highlights a challenge with socializing for autistic people: We sometimes struggle to anticipate reactions, as well as understand and use jokes.

Another problem that I had in primary school, being the odd and challenging student, was the teachers sitting me at the naughty kid's destructive table. There they taught me to understand a lot more about sexual physiology than I really wanted to at that age because the naughty kids were just full of colorful language and interesting insults. This group of kids took advantage of my vulnerability and were acting like bullies. I am sure many autistic people like you have also experienced this time after time at school and work.

But on the plus side, eventually the school then made a designated desk for me and the only other special-needs kid, who had schizophrenia.

While sitting and working at the desk next to this kid, I did learn that he had problems, and I was vastly different from not only him but different from everyone else in the school. That was a challenging time for me, I felt alienated from my peers, and I thought that the teachers really didn't understand me at all.

I know many people will say that they had a bad experience at school. Still, I honestly think the lost generation that really missed out was the one attending school when that whole, you know, early '80s to mid-90s period of autism diagnosis was not accessible in our part of the world.

Masking Pros and Cons

When you're undiagnosed, you have somewhat of an "Oh man, I have to swim, or I'm going to sink and just become a socially awkward mess" battle every day. My parents didn't help me personally in that aspect. They just wanted me to get on with it, so I had to figure out a way to swim on my own. Kind of like, it's your first time swimming and you end up being thrown into a shark tank. Thanks, mum!

Letting me swim solo in primary school made that experience one of the most challenging times in my life. I had to try to not only learn the things that my teachers were teaching me, but I also had to try and exist in an environment where people found me quite odd and unusual. So how do you swim in an environment where you're drowning?

You copy the motherfucking shit out of someone who's doing it well!

I literally watched movies and TV shows back-to-back as soon as I got home from school to learn more about social interactions. I'd watch *Saved by the Bell* or *Sabrina the Teenage Witch*. I'd watch Star Wars too of course. Then I'd have a look at how the characters talked, like A.C. Slater and Han Solo. I'd observe how they interacted with their friends, and I mimicked some of the words. I still do this to this day. I find that I model myself a lot on my American idols and copy their expressions, actions, and mannerisms, trying to present myself as "normal" using their personality traits. And this, my friends, as some of you may already know, is masking.

For those of you reading that are unfamiliar with autistic masking, it is basically a way in which you pretend to be a character in a social situation to survive it.

Imagine you want your friends to accept you. One night, they all want to go out for pizza, but you don't because the sensory input from the pizza place is too much for you. You're masking if you just agree to go along to the pizza place, pretending you are ok with the situation when really you just want to avoid it.

Typically, people say that masking is a bad thing because it impacts your diagnosis process, as it can make it challenging to understand what is symptomatic and what is masking, what's real and what's not. As you can tell, this makes the entire diagnosis process more challenging for you to access support because people don't know how you genuinely act in certain situations.

But on the contrary, masking can be used as a survival technique, and I feel all humans have to mask at one point or another. If you're in a situation where you need to fit in, you will pretend to be like the other people; this is masking, and people do this every single day.

So, my primary technique for surviving school and swimming through the sharks was masking myself as a shark. That way, I went a little bit unnoticed and sometimes felt sheltered until the other sharks noticed me.

Do you know I run a weekly live Instagram show on this topic every Monday night on IG Live? You can go and check it out @TheAspieworld, if you haven't already followed me. The show is called *Mask Off Monday*, and I talk to guests on the autism spectrum about how they mask, how they've managed to do what they do, and how they survive all the time with masking. But one of the biggest things I do is ask them if they believe masking is a good thing or a bad thing. After reviewing all the pros and cons of masking, you'll just need to decide for yourself if that workaround is right for you.

Implement Twenty Minute Sensory Breaks

I first discovered the benefits of sensory breaks when my teachers *locked me in the classroom on my own*. Yes, this is completely illegal, but it was a wild time in the late '80s, early '90s. Why would they do this? I couldn't go outside to play at playtime, and I couldn't go to the swimming pool when the school made the trip to one. Locked up (with an actual lock and key), I had no way of getting out and was all alone for an hour while the teachers took the rest of the kids from my class swimming at the local swimming pool.

I've no idea how they got away with this and how my parents never sued them, but nevertheless, they haven't. Regardless, I really enjoyed the time on my own during the school day. Although I didn't know it at the time, this was actually a sensory break, a way of creating a break from the sensory input I experienced throughout the school day.

This enforced sensory break highlighted that I thrived from having sensory breaks during my working day at school. I use this as the number one hack to get the most out of my day without burning out. My advice? Try to put small 20- to 30-minute sensory breaks into your day; this works well if you are at work or a stay-at-home person. The relevant gap creates a sensory decompression.

Right now, put this book down, open your diary or calendar on your phone, and schedule 20 minutes of time today so you can sit in silence with no sensory input (or as little as you can create). Honestly, this is going to make you feel so incredible.

Now that I think about it, being in mainstream schools without support, aka being dropped in the deep end, was good for me in some ways with language and social interaction. I had to learn the jargon of each social group. I had to learn many things about other people's mannerisms and social constructs fast. And although this was scary at times, the outcome was that I am more confident around people now because of this, which I believe I would not have been if I had attended an SEN (Special Education Needs) school.

Actionable Takeaway Points

- Learn to recognize the challenges you face in communicating, learning, and socializing.

- Masking can be useful in certain situations, so decide when and how you wish to use it.

- Give yourself twenty to thirty minutes of silence throughout your day; these sensory breaks will work wonders for your life.

- Try to look at the challenges you've experienced and the things you have learned because of them in a positive light. Your experiences have made you who you are, and that's powerful. This mindset will build confidence.

Chapter Six

Autism and the Workplace: Revealing the Honest Truth About Autistic Employment

Autism and employment, that's enough said, wouldn't you agree? Working is something we all want to do, because that's how we live our lives, and autistic people are no different in this respect.

However, working environments can be super challenging for autistic people like us. From the lighting in office buildings and warehouses to the sounds and smells of equipment, people, and even breakroom lunches, there are so many potential triggers for our sensory processing issues.

So, it's no wonder that employment for autistic people can be a negative experience, if there is an experience at all. I bet you have worked many different jobs, or at least tried your hand at them, over the years. Perhaps you felt like you could do them, but then they ended in ways you didn't see coming. This is all completely normal for us autistic people.

I am now the owner of my own company, and I LOVE the work that I do, but it wasn't always like that. I have worked in many roles, from ice cream man all the way to tech support, remotely fixing computers in Australia in the middle of the night. However, not one of those jobs could support and accommodate me fully.

There are many reasons for this, as I discuss in this chapter, but retrospectively I've realized how I could have made those jobs autism friendly so they were, at the very least, bearable. But that is the collateral hit that one takes being the test subject in life as an autistic person trying out the working world.

Luckily for you, these reflections and discoveries can provide you with ways to improve your working experience and career success. This chapter covers everything that I wish I had known before entering the working world, so you will have all the best hacks I wish I could have had.

My First Job

My first job was as a paper boy, like any other humble teenager starting in the world of work.

Why was I a paper boy? My parents told me when I was 14 that I needed to get a job, which was ironic because, at that time, my father was unemployed. He was also refusing to become employed again because he was somewhat ashamed about his business going under, losing his house, and his business being repossessed by the bank.

Regardless, my father told me that I needed to get a job that would be somewhat sustainable, so I asked my friends in school, and they said, "Yeah, get a paper route, and it will be awesome."

Probably the most interesting thing about being an autistic kid and having a paper route is the perk of just being able to deliver a paper in the middle of the night. Okay, not actually night, but it was like starting a shift at 5:30 in the morning and nobody was around.

My usual day was walking to the paper shop where I picked up a bunch of papers, putting a sack across my chest like a messenger bag, and heading off.

For the next hour, I was delivering papers to people's letter-boxes on a Sunday morning. It was good, although the pay was 100 percent ridiculous. The perks were that I was able to please my parents' demands and did not have to deal face-to-face with anybody. The downside was I soon grew bored of the early, dark mornings and being wet and soaked through when it rained. That look didn't go well for me as I navigated through teenage life.

So, when I was about 16, I realized that I needed a real job that paid more than a paper route because everyone has jobs. Every 16-year-old wants to get a job and wants to try and do something.

I asked my friend Martyn, whom I was pretty friendly with because we were in computer class and he was somewhat of a Pokémon enthusiast. He told me that his uncle owned ice cream vans, and on the sunny Welsh coast of North Wales, there is an abundance of those. I pleased my parents again and got a job as an ice cream man.

That was my first encounter dealing with customers head-on, face-to-face. And oh my goodness, it didn't go well. I literally did one day of ice cream van work, and I instantly regretted it. I said no, enough is enough, and quit. One of my biggest concerns was people's predetermined ideas of what they think an ice cream man should be like. I was dry, to the point, quite logical, and quite literal, and they didn't like this.

My biggest takeaway from my first two jobs though was coming away with a greater sense of self-confidence. Now I knew for sure that I could do something in the working world. I was not (as I had previously thought) useless. Autistic people sometimes feel inferior to others, especially at a young age when they see other peers getting jobs and doing paper routes. Holding down these jobs, even briefly, gave me the boost I needed to feel like I can accomplish normal-life things. So, my advice to you is to put yourself out there. Do a job that may not be for you, but proves that you can exist in the working environment and you are in control of your life.

Socializing and Work

A lot of people enjoy what we like to call "Small Talk." Oh, I know you shuddered as you read that last line.

They should rename it "The Terrifying Time" because "Small Talk" is when people talk about stuff to you and then you have to respond to them. The talk has to be something you have nothing in common with, and somehow you have to create conversation from this.

In life, especially at work, people will talk about things that don't matter, like the importance of the weather and the disregard for the bus service. All of these things have no natural common ground with anybody, so I have a motto: If it's not worth saying, I won't bother saying it. That's my golden rule for small talk survival! People do not always initiate the conversation when small talk is imminent, but if they do, just use kindness and honesty in your simple response. If a person asks if you have been busy or up to much, you can be honest and tell them. If you want to try to initiate small talk, then only speak of valuable offerings. This means if you have value to offer a situation via knowledge, then speak it.

Disclosing Diagnosis at Work: The Problems of Autism Honesty

As you know, we autistic people have an inbuilt moralistic oath to always be 100 percent honest because if you're not genuine, then you're not being true. If you are not being true, you're pretending and pretending is not who you are, so why wouldn't you be honest? I know this doesn't make sense to many people, but to the autistic individuals reading this book, a heads up: You are qualified to know that the inside of my brain is exactly like yours.

But does honesty about your autism diagnosis help or hurt you when it comes to employment? I think it is a good point to discuss the pros and cons of an autism diagnosis, as this question has its moment when trying to find work.

The good thing about having an official diagnosis of autism is that you will be able to access support and help from your local authorities and programs that work to support autistic people. This can also be true in employment and education where reasonable adjustments can be made to help you have more success in your role.

However, your diagnosis could also be turned against you if the employer is uneducated in autism or thinks your diagnosis could be negative for the company.

A friend of mine actually was offered five jobs that she had applied for, but upon disclosing to the employers that she had a diagnosis of autism, each one of the five positions she had been offered suddenly vanished. You see, some employers see that autism could impact your ability to work, which then impacts their company and so forth. However, it is a very narrow-minded view that discounts the potential of an autistic person by focusing only on the negatives of autism and not the positives.

This experience taught my friend to first look at legality and legal rulings on disability support and duty of care. To overcome this hurdle, she only disclosed that she had autism after they decided that she was the right candidate for the role. After she started working, she asked for some additional support as needed. You don't have to tell anyone about your diagnosis upfront. You only need to disclose your issues if you are in need of access.

Now, because of our honesty, this next part is not easy either. Responding to interview questions with blunt honesty can be costly. Most jobs require you to be great with people skills from the get-go. They want you to be a very confident person walking into an interview, to be able to talk the talk and walk into work and tell them everything excellent about you as an individual.

Unfortunately for autistic individuals, we often respond too honestly and literally. For example, an interviewer might ask, "Do you have flaws?" I am 100 percent going to answer something like: "Yeah, my OCD is terrible; it makes me very late for everything in life." As one can imagine, this kind of response does not paint me in a good light, so interviews didn't go well for me, and I was utterly stuck.

I couldn't get a job this way. The world is set up to go against autistic individuals because the global economic market wants a specific type of person. The entire frame of employment is built around neurotypical individuals. Everything from the way that they set up interviews, the questions, the tasks they ask you to do, right down to if you eventually get the job and find out the environment is not autism friendly. Desks are always cluttered with cables and equipment, there is a high noise volume in offices and factories, and lighting in many places of work is not ideal for those of us with sensory issues.

It doesn't stop there though. The idea of shift work and an ever-changing weekly rotation can really play with an autistic person's ability to place themselves in a good routine; as we all know, we autistics love routines.

So how did I break this mold? You see, us autistic individuals are very clever; we problem solve.

The Agency Work-Around

Before I get into how I hacked this little system initially, remember that friend I mentioned whose job offers were rescinded? She's a very dear friend of mine and fellow YouTuber / Instagram influencer who goes by the name of Anna Moomin. Once the employers asked if she had any special requirements, and she told them she had autism, suddenly the work dried up, and she was no longer accepted in a position.

I really wanted to fight this cause on my YouTube channel and my social media, so in 2020, just before the global pandemic, I briefed the European Parliament in France on the deficit of autistic individuals in work and the current awful state of employment for autistic people. They listened well. I hope that they took some action from what I said and that they can relate to the story about my friend Anna, which was sad, to say the least.

While I hope my efforts help others avoid Anna's struggles in the future, let's get back to that hack I mentioned that could help you now. How did Dan hack the employment industry? Well, as I'm sure you have realized by now, I love computers. However, I didn't have any qualifications. So I thought, well how am I going to get in with a company to allow me to fix computers, when A) I can't do an interview and B) I can't go there with any qualifications or credentials that would allow me to walk right into the job?

I realized that if I started work at an agency that only works with IT (information technology) clients, I may have a chance. Work agencies don't really care about your qualifications or educational background. All the agency wants is people in positions to fill a place because that's how they get money. They fill roles for larger companies that then reward them monetarily, and the individual is placed in work. This is kind of a whole cycle.

This goes for all of us autistic individuals reading this and wanting to get into a work field. Find an agency, or a volunteer group, or an internship with a company or organization that is in your ideal career path. Use that as leverage to gain experience. This worked brilliantly for me as I outline here.

I approached a work agency and asked if I could get any work as a computer person or something IT related. Well, what do you know? I was given a position fixing gaming computers remotely from an office in the city next to where I lived.

I could travel in the morning, go there and fix computers remotely without telephone work, and then duck out.

Unfortunately for me, this all sounded good until I was given a permanent contract with the company because they realized that I was of excellent value to them; they then said, "Can you take some phone calls?" I ended up on a hot desk.

This did not go well, and I had my first at-work meltdown.

I decided that this wasn't for me when I approached the manager and found that they were pretty reluctant to help. I went back to the office and told my boss I couldn't do this anymore. They listened and allowed me to fix computers in Australia and America overnight, so I was just at work at 11 p.m. and finished at 7 a.m., which was fantastic.

I could do this and there was nobody in the office, not a soul, just a huge open office and me. I was able to fix computers at my leisure, and the only phone calls I had to do were once a night with an Australian engineer for me to ship out new parts to them. Easy peasy—I could do it very easily.

However, this job didn't last long because they changed my hours to a seven-day rotor system work. I'd be doing night work another day, then doing daytime work on telephones, so they went back on the deal. I didn't like this and decided that it wasn't for me.

Luckily, because I had the experience of working there through my placement at the work agency, I could then go to another job with experience, and this was worth more than qualifications.

Recognizing a Need for Diagnosis

My first meltdown was only one sign that I'd need more help finding a suitable career. The next job I had was working for a large American healthcare finance company. The cool thing about it was that I was dealing with financial reconciliation reports daily, which basically meant numbers. Numbers are comfortable, numbers are fantastic, and I loved it. However, problems started to appear; more signs that I'd need a change and support.

The nine-to-five constant office chatter, uncomfortable clothes, seats near strangers, late nights spent fixing problems that other people created: It all dragged on me.

I developed a severe case of depression and was put on anti-depressant medication for the first time. This stuff made me a zombie, and the work made me sadder and sadder.

Luckily for me, the company went bust and moved to a different country; they made me redundant and gave me a nice severance package, which was quite handy. But I had only scratched the surface of my career issues, as I still had not been diagnosed and could not fully understand how to help myself at this point.

After the healthcare company went bust, I then started working at a multimedia company for five years, where I had the biggest meltdown of my life. In 2014, I was employed by a local multimedia company that did a lot of international work and was very small. I managed to get this job because of my previous experience.

There were maybe five people in the whole company in my office, and they were pretty young, pretty cool, and interested in things I liked too: Dungeons & Dragons, computer games, Pokémon, and stuff like that.

The company sadly grew rapidly, expanding to over two hundred employees, and this meant only one thing: We had to move to a new office.

Now while this expansion was happening, I had been sitting in the same chair in the same office for the past three years, and life was going okay. I was dealing with it. No anxiety because it was a small office, and no depression because I didn't have the hassle from other people doing the job incorrectly.

When the company decided to move offices, I was actually away on vacation. I came back to my desk, and it had been moved; everything was in the wrong place, and I just freaked out.

I had a huge meltdown in the office, panicking. The managers quickly put me into another room and locked the door so that people could not come in and be nosy. They asked if I was okay, but I was not. I could not even drive. I was in such a mess that my girlfriend came to pick me up. At home, I had a post-meltdown realization: The world is not designed for my brain, and I couldn't do this anymore. I ended up down another dark path of depression, upset detachment, and just complete and utter despair.

I enrolled in therapy, and I was doing a psychotherapy counselling course. As I was in therapy, they wanted to test me for all kinds of things, and autism was on the list. I went to a specialist, and then I was diagnosed with autism spectrum disorder (ASD); at the time it was called Asperger syndrome, but we now call it ASD.

That was the defining moment for me in my life and every-thing comes to this.

So, I looked at myself and thought again that I couldn't do this anymore. But this time, the thought that followed was that I needed to do something else, so I decided that I was going to do two things. First, I was going to quit work and get trained in something that I enjoy to please my brain and my lifelong obsession with being a scientist. This is when I pursued my degree in chemistry, and even did all kinds of science before getting my degree.

Chemistry was just amazing, and I'm so glad I did that, but there was still the second thing I promised to myself: I would create a job for myself and work for myself because I was not happy working for somebody else.

I couldn't deal with the pressure issues of listening to some-body give me a verbal commands list with no guidance, prioritization, or clear linear projection.

I did some odd bits and pieces while doing my chemistry degree, which stemmed from marketing a toy company to monthly Geek subscription boxes. I also was chief editor at a magazine that went into the subscription boxes.

I taught myself how to build websites and got into social media management. But one of the things that I was doing on the side was making videos on YouTube about my journey, about my struggles with autism and all the things that come into it.

So, without me planning it, my YouTube channel just took off. I started to be able to do less work for other people in terms of website design and social media management, and do more work on YouTube and actually get paid for helping people directly.

Now it wasn't an awful lot to begin with, but it was something of an incentive, and I was like, "Yes, I can do this." That is how I got started with my career on YouTube.

Choosing a Career

So how can you get started on your own career? First off, know that you got this, and you can do anything you want. Even though the process sucked at first, I did it.

Autistic people have major issues with conventional jobs and career markets. We think outside the box, so you'll need a career that supports that. Here are a few ways to create strong career ideas and job opportunities:

- Hone in on your talent and pursue it (go to classes, events, etc).

- Build or create work experiences around your special interest.

- Pursue career advice and opportunities around your special interests (this could be anything at all, as there are so many ways to create a career now with social media and the Internet).

There's lots to digest through my employment journey, but I hope the following takeaway points help you hack the employment world too.

Actionable Takeaway Points

- Put yourself out there in the working world, even if it's not always an ideal job, to prove that you can do it. Boost that confidence!

- Remember that problem-solving is an autism strength and an employer's desire.

- Create opportunities by working backwards from the goal, just like I did with the agency. Experience is greater than qualifications in many jobs.

- Self-employment is a good way to get started as an income for autistic people, as you can use your obsessive interest to turn it into an educational outlet.

Chapter Seven

Special Interests: Using Your Autistic Brain to Manage Your Life

We as autistic people get worried, stressed, and anxious about so many things. But we can decrease the anxiety in our lives with the workaround tips and hacks I share in this chapter.

I have struggled through a lot of anxiety and meltdowns in my life, but the times when I was able to overcome these situations were like lightbulb moments for me. I repeated my strategies to see if they would work again. They work so well that I decided to write them down and give these secrets to you.

If you need more calm and less anxiety in your life, then this chapter is for you.

Special Interests Are a Strength

Special interests, often called "Obsessive Interests," are an integral part of life for people on the autism spectrum. We, as autistic individuals, all have unique special interests that may seem odd to others. Still, they are equally as fascinating to people who know why we are so fascinated by the subject of interest.

We will all have an obsessive interest in certain areas because our brains work in a way that pushes us to intricately look at something specific and understand its beauty, no matter what it is.

I had heard of a gentleman, through my ASD support worker, who was obsessed with Marilyn Monroe. He was so interested in her that he'd been to Marilyn Monroe's house in the United States; he knew everything about it. He had watched all the documentaries and read all the books about her life. He was just obsessed with her life and who she was. This was all not in a lustful way. He was intrigued by how her life played out, why she died so young, who was involved with everything that took place, and all the pieces of her puzzle.

Now, when the general public thinks about autism, they talk about people who are good at puzzles. Well, while I am good at puzzles, not everyone on the spectrum is good at general puzzles. However, we know that we like to problem solve. I hear you, my autistic family! I see you trying to make sense of the world and all of its complexities. This is because we are problem solving from the get-go!

My obsessions started when I was a young child. I always wanted to live in a virtual reality environment because of the current state of the world and the horrors that shocked me beyond the usual struggles of being an autistic individual who finds it hard to be in the world.

I just wanted to have some escapism from the mundane or neurotypical world, which is socially constructed and complex for the autistic individuals living in it.

I began to research virtual reality, robots, and computing. I used to stay indoors all day, fascinated with robots I saw on TV and in magazines. I was so taken by virtual reality and computers. I tried to learn how to build virtual reality programs from shows on television, documentaries, websites, books, and anything I could get my hands on to teach me about virtual reality.

I tried to make something like this myself. In the early '90s, virtual reality was shocking, and the only experience I had was in the Birmingham or Wolverhampton town library. There was an exhibition to show how a drop of water travels through the water system and irrigation pipes, and they did this via an old-school Virtuality headset. Oh yes, one of those bad boys that was like having a TV screen strapped to your head!

I knew from that moment that this was my main obsession. I loved it. If we fast forward to today, my team and I here at The Aspie World all meet in virtual reality, and we all have Meta Quest headsets. We are building our community environment within virtual reality, so it's nice to know that I never lost my passion for VR.

However, my special interests grew with me. Over time, I was fascinated by science and space and everything technology-wise, which eventually motivated me to get my degree in chemistry.

I've also grown to love trying to figure out geo-economic world politics, how governments move, and why governments do what they do. This interest actually led me down the path of wanting to understand mysteries and puzzles; one of my top mystery obsessions, as morbid as it may be, is the 9/11 terror attacks that happened in the United States of America. This, to me, is a big puzzle because there are many, many scientific and other inconsistencies that I would like to figure out, but that is for another book!

So why are obsessive interests good for autistic people? If we break it down, it all comes down to a very simple desire to engage in a problem-solving process whenever we are confronted with a problem.

What we are confronted with is actually a potential toward a solution. A problem is a negative feeling, but a solution is a positive feeling, and we always want to go away from pain toward pleasure. Negative is pain; positive is pleasure. So, when we problem solve and complete the solution on a task, we feel the pleasure that we have resolved something in a positive light.

The autistic brain is constantly chasing dopamine, and you get a release of dopamine when you problem solve. This is the basic principle of why autistic individuals are obsessed with things. We find the complexities in things, and it's those complexities and their solutions that we love to chase for dopamine.

Now here's the funny thing about problems: Everybody can learn from the autistic mind when it comes to facing problems. Most people are scared of problems. Why are people scared of problems? Because problems create worry, and worry creates anxiety. But there's something precious in the way autistic people see problems. We can actually help anybody if we know what the opposite of the negative they are experiencing is, which would be a positive.

We know that we need to avoid negativity and go toward positivity. If we know that something is a problem, we know that there is a solution for that problem, or we wouldn't even see it as a problem.

It's kind of like if you are driving on the road you want to get from A to B; however, there is a boulder in the middle of the road, causing you to stop. You know that the boulder stopping you from moving forward could be solved by removing the boulder or moving it to the side to make way for your car. This is more of a potential toward a solution than it is a problem.

So the question stands, is it a problem or a potential toward a solution? If what we are faced with is potential toward the solution and actually not a problem at all, then there's no need for anxiety.

People often forget that they already know the answer to their problems. They just think that problems are there and that's it. There are no solutions. But, a problem can't exist without a solution, just like dark is to light, positive to negative. One cannot exist without the other. You have to have a solution. Autistic individuals instinctively know this and strive toward finding the solution.

Hydrate During a Meltdown

Even with our special interests and problem-solving strengths, there will be times when we are overwhelmed. Well, when autistic individuals are faced with burnouts, meltdowns, or shutdowns, it feels like a complete and utter catastrophic event is happening in our lives. The event may be tiny and insignificant to the onlooker, but this is very much a big deal and can impact the autistic person's life.

Sometimes, when you can stop in your tracks during a difficult time, just before you hit meltdown level, you can avoid the meltdown entirely by enjoying the subject of your obsessive interest. You will begin to drip dopamine, so the crisis is averted.

Even if you can't avoid the meltdown, the dopamine can still help you feel better faster and recover quicker from the meltdown. Many ask me, "How do I recover from a meltdown?" I simply recommend drinking water and staying hydrated. Your brain is using a lot of energy and going through lots of oxygen in the water to pump adrenaline around your body when you are stressed, worried, or anxious. Drinking water stops your body from being dehydrated and feeling worse and sluggish after a meltdown.

Change Your Environment

In addition to hydrating, another thing you need to do is instantly change your environment when you are experiencing the meltdown. Switch from the "pain environment" to a pleasurable, safe one that you can control, preferably surrounded by your special interest.

For example, if you are in a theater and you are anxious, the noise increases, and the overall sensory input creates havoc, sending you down the path of a potential meltdown. You can instantly walk outside or to your car, where you can control the temperature, the smells, the amount of noise, and the people around you. But most importantly, you can have your tablet or phone with you to search for and look at your obsessive interest because, again, this releases dopamine.

Taking this step moves you away from pain and toward pleasure; it's coming from a triggering environment and putting yourself into a controlled non-triggering environment.

I do this daily, and it is the most significant help I can suggest to stop a meltdown from occurring.

Special Interests Can Divert a Meltdown

While I mentioned this briefly in the last two examples, I really can't stress enough how your special interest can be the perfect diversion for meltdown recovery. You can see this strategy in action in the second season of a TV show I was involved with. The show is called *Atypical* by the Netflix production company.

In the show, it follows the life of an autistic young adult called Sam as he navigates his way through life as a teenager on the spectrum. It covers his life's ups and downs with girls, a job, and everything in between.

His topic of interest was penguins in Antarctica and other animals on that continent, so when he's having a meltdown in one of the episodes, his sister comforts him and puts his headphones on him, then starts talking to him about emperor penguins.

Instantly, Sam feels like a dopamine hit has just been given to him and starts to relax.

This is a fantastic example of how just talking about your particular interest, researching it, or being around your special interest can help you overcome many difficulties in your day-to-day life.

Actionable Takeaway Points

- Your special interest is a strength, so value it and cultivate it.

- Hydrate yourself if you are having a meltdown.

- Remove yourself from the environment that triggers a meltdown. Put yourself in a controlled, safe space for recovery.

- Use your special interest as a diversion to come around from a meltdown quicker.

Chapter Eight

Your Future: Making a Solid Plan to Support Your Needs

Autism doesn't stop at eighteen.

There seems to be so much child support or young teen support set up for autistic individuals, but there's less to none for the older, aging autistic population.

This really worries me, and I will not allow our community to suffer if I can help.

How many times have you said to someone that you are autistic, and they say the most inappropriate things: "You don't look autistic" or "My friend's kid is autistic, and you are not like him" or even "Well, if you are, then you must be very high-functioning."

This kind of rhetoric is very dismissive of autistic people and can make us feel like imposters trying to prove to someone a condition that we have.

This chapter outlines so many life, finance, workplace, and learning hacks to create a more stable and successful future for you. Take this as a guide to better your life moving forward so you can really make the most out of it and succeed as your own self-advocate for your own condition.

You can do anything as long as you have the correct tools, and that's what I am providing here: the tools you need.

The Changing Landscape for Autistic People

I recently did a podcast with my friend and fellow autistic, Thomas Henley, who runs a podcast called the *Thoughtie Auti*, which is a cool name; dang, I wish I had thought of this!

On the show, we discussed a lot of the advocacy I do for autism on my social media channels, and then I asked him what content he makes and why he got started. I asked why because it is always important to me to know the driving force behind people's decisions to advocate for something; this shows me their true colors and feelings on topics.

Thomas stated that he wanted to start this podcast and his Instagram account because of the information he had read on the age of death of the average autistic person. It was somewhere around thirty to forty for high support needs autistic individuals, and then fifty to sixty for lower support needs individuals like myself and Thomas.

Wow, this shocked me to my core! This was one of the first times I think I was speechless.

I asked him why this was so; these figures cannot be accurate, can they? Thomas replied with a logical statement that backed up much of the research I had been doing up until that point on the future of autistic people and their long-term life help and support plans. He stated that many autistic individuals are so worried about their future and how to keep and create a better standard of living that it is overwhelming.

This worried me, as I know the potential in all of us autistic individuals is so unique. We have so much to offer the world, and we need to make sure we are on track to do all the things that we are put here to do. The world is indeed set up to be neurotypically friendly, and not accommodative to autistic individuals. That is just how it is; however, it doesn't have to stay like that.

There has been a big shift in how companies and organizations now look at how they operate and make accommodations for individuals of all abilities.

The National Autistic Society here in the U.K. created a campaign for "Autism Hour" in supermarkets to create a more sensory-friendly environment. This started as a monthly thing, but now it has grown into a weekly thing and what I believe will be a global implementation across all shops within the next five years.

In 2020, I briefed the European Union on the devastating deficit of autistic individuals out of work in the U.K. alone. I discussed how we can create a better and more accepting work environment and interview process to give everyone the opportunity for employment.

We have moved away from autism awareness to autism understanding and acceptance. With more information available for everyone about autism and its impact on autistic people's lives, how can they help and support autistic people?

But we have to understand that all future aspirations of a more neurodiverse, understanding world will have to be a joint effort. It is 50 percent the things I have already mentioned, but it also has to be 50 percent input and effort from you as a representative of our community.

Wondering how to get started? I have created lists and information below to help you play your part in the future we all see and need. These are basic groundwork that will help you grow as an autistic person and also create a solid independent living foundation that you can use to become more of a self-advocate.

Life Skills

Having life skills is something that all people learn over time, but it is worth noting these tips and hacks to help set you up for independent life as an autistic person.

SHOPPING

- Using apps like Bring! will help with a visual representation of what you need to buy at the store and is available on all devices.

- Remember to take sunglasses and noise-cancelling headphones with you when shopping to create your sensory environment.

APPOINTMENTS AND REMINDERS

- Use visual calendars on your wall where you put stickers, draw a picture, or write what appointments you have coming up. Hang it so you can see it every day.

- When making appointments, always opt-in or ask them to send you an email, text, or call reminder of your appointment.

- You can use apps like Reminders or your digital assistant (Alexa, Google, or Siri) to remind you to go to appointments.

UTILITIES

- Inform your energy suppliers of your disabilities as they have special early priority alert systems for disabled people, so you are first to know of any faults, etc.

Managing Finances

Managing money is a difficult concept for a lot of us on the autism spectrum, but there are ways to keep on top of this.

REAL WORLD

- Assign a family member as your finance helper.

- Talk to your bank about your needs so they can set up triggers and limits on spending, etc.

- Use online banking apps, as they have visual representations of expenditures.

- Use visual charts with envelopes on them with labels like Bills, Savings, Food, etc. This can give you a full visual and physical structure to finance. You can also set this up on your online banking apps.

APPS

- Zeny is a simple accounting app that helps you input money coming in and money going out and gives you visual images of where your money is going. ($20 a year)

- You can use Google Drive / Google Sheets as part of the Google Docs free online software to make spreadsheets to track your income and outgoings. This is a free and easy way to keep on top of money.

MONEY SAFETY

- Having a friend or family member who will do a monthly check on finances makes sure bills are being paid and that you are not spending money on gambling, scams, etc.

- Ask your bank to set up an alarm for gambling and behavior checking so that if something odd happens to your money, you are alerted and the bank freezes the transactions.

Workplace Accommodations

When going into the workplace, the environment can be challenging for autistic people. Therefore, these are the things that must be covered when starting a career.

REASONABLE ADJUSTMENTS

- Ask for access to a sensory muted space (could be clean, organized desk, use of computer only, no pens, etc).

- Ask for smaller meetings, so they're not too overwhelming.

- Ask for allowance of sensory breaks (if needed).

- Come to an agreement on a consistent start and end time of lunch so it can be a strict routine.

- Ask for sunglasses and headphones to be allowed in the workplace.

EMPLOYER INPUT

- Ask for, or find an autism work champion who you can talk to if you need help with anything, including communicating your needs to the company.

- Inform them that you may need instructions in a visual format, not just a list or ad-hoc conversations.

- Remind them of their duty of care to make sure you are in good mental health.

Learning Environment Accommodations

Autistic individuals need help while in any learning environment. As such, I have listed the best ways to create full productivity out of any learning environment to make it autism suitable.

- Create a personal learner plan (this will include different start and end times, any additional requirements, fidget toys, etc).

- Make a pre-class visit to see and explore the class before the term starts.

- Request reasonable adjustments: use of computer in exams, extra time in exams, ability to use headphones and sunglasses in class, etc.

- Organize paper handouts daily by labeling with the date and page numbers.

- Use an iPad in class for communicating and dictating; also you can use it to audio record lessons to refer to when reviewing.

- Have a mentor who you can consult for advice and general communication every week.

- Ask for access to quiet rooms and the use of sensory items in class.

Glossary

ADHD: A neurological condition commonly diagnosed with autism; it presents issues with focus and attentiveness. More often than not, it comes with hyperactivity and massive amounts of anxiety.

Aspergers: A term used to describe autistic people of lower support needs. Named after the controversial research of Hans Asperger from 1942, it has been used as a diagnostic term for autism since the 1980s. Asperger syndrome now falls under the broader label "Autism spectrum disorder" as of 2013.

Autism Level 1–3: Autism is now diagnosed more widely on variant levels from Autism Spectrum Disorder Level 1 to Autism Spectrum Disorder Level 3.

Autistic: An individual affected by autism or autism spectrum disorder, which is a neurodiverse disorder marked by impairments in the ability to communicate, motor development, and social interaction. There is also a presence of repetitive behaviors or special interests.

Autistics: More than one individual affected by autism or autism spectrum disorder.

Burnout: A form of exhaustion caused by a constant feeling of being swamped. It is a result of excessive and prolonged emotional, physical, and mental stress. Burnout happens when you're overwhelmed, emotionally drained, and unable to keep up with life's incessant demands.

High Support Needs: An autistic person who needs large amounts of support to function day-to-day, from getting dressed to eating and communicating.

Hypersensitivity: Overly stimulated by sensory input: Lights are too bright, smells are intense, and noises are too loud.

Hyposensitivity: The opposite of hypersensitivity, this condition causes a person to have a lower-than-average response to sensory input, such as a low sense of smell or touch or even slow sense of hearing without any biological hearing issues.

Low Support Needs: A person on the autism spectrum but doesn't need as much daily support as other autistic individuals. They can maneuver around everyday life with low support.

Masking: Hiding your authentic self in an effort to gain greater social acceptance. The costs of camouflaging your true personality and emotions can add up exponentially, causing you to experience a sense of loss, anxiety, and depression.

Meltdown: A reaction to feeling overwhelmed. It's typically not something an individual can control. Lots of situations can trigger meltdowns, and the triggers vary by person. For example, pain, fear, or unexpected changes to routines, as well as life situations like a breakup or job loss, can cause meltdowns.

Obsessive Interests: A special topic of interest field in which an autistic individual is obsessed and will research for hours, talk about nonstop, and collect everything there is to collect on this topic.

Sensory Processing Disorder: The experience of having too much sensory input, or not enough. This could be too many noises or smells coming into your system and overloading you at once, or it could be the opposite where you cannot hear people or sounds around you.

Stim, stimming: The word "stim" is an abbreviation for "stimming," or "self-stimulatory," a word which refers to the repetition of body movements, words, sounds, or movement of objects by individuals on the spectrum. It is one of the most obvious characteristics and is one of the diagnostic criteria for autism.

The Spectrum: A spectrum is a broad range of similar things or qualities, like the wide spectrum of political beliefs. Spectrum in terms of autism relates to the scale of support needs and life impact. On one side of the spectrum, you can have people diagnosed with terms like Asperger's syndrome, ADHD, and high-functioning autism. These are all diagnoses with minimal support needed. The other side of the spectrum can have a diagnosis of non-verbal autism, savant syndrome, and co-occurring intellectual disabilities co-occurring in there. This would mean they are at a higher support needs level and require more assistance.

Acknowledgments

I would like to thank everyone at Page Street Publishing for their belief in me creating this awesome book; you are all awesome.

I'd like to thank every one of my friends and family who have supported me in my wild ideas to start a YouTube channel, write a book, and create coaching programs; their support means so much to me.

My fans are the biggest supporters I have. Their endless support and cheerleading of my work and projects is the reason I can do what I do and help everyone that I help.

I would like to thank every single one of you who has followed me on social media, commented, liked a post, and shared my work. YOU have made the world a better place, and we are only just getting started.

Thank you for reading this book.

About the Author

Daniel M. Jones, most notably known as The Aspie World, is, at the time of writing this, the biggest autistic social media influencer on the Internet.

Daniel has been working in the field of autism education and influence since 2013 when he was diagnosed with autism, ADHD, OCD, and dyslexia.

Not knowing where to find information in video format that was digestible and informative on autism, he started the YouTube channel The Aspie World to help inform, educate, and entertain people about autism and co-occurring conditions. Boasting over 200,000 subscribers on his YouTube channel and over 200,000 more across all other social media channels, The Aspie World has won WEGO Health and YouTube awards and has been nominated for Autism Professional Awards by the National Autistic Society.

Since the conception of his YouTube channel, Daniel has briefed the EU Parliament on autism and the employment gap, graduated from MIT on digital leadership for disabilities, and created the first-ever neurodiverse panel at VidCon U.S., the largest online video conference in the world.

Daniel has appeared on TV across the globe and in many magazines, helping promote the understanding of autism to a large audience. This includes appearing at events as a keynote speaker in London, Spain, and LA.

He also has worked closely with The National Autistic Society in the U.K. on many campaigns and fundraisers they have done and has a working relationship with the U.K. NHS autism teams.

Daniel is currently working with the Autism Wales national team to create support opportunities for autistic individuals in Wales, and he's working with charities in Canada to set up events there for autistic families.

Among all these things, Daniel and The Aspie World have grown to help events like The Paralympics, represent Google on Autism Awareness, and create educational courses and membership coaching programs via the website www.TheAspieWorld.com.

Daniels's mission is to foster an understanding of autism to create a better world for all autistic people and their families and connected relatives.

Index

A

I

J

L

M

U

V

W

Warhammer Pointing Club, 52

Weebles, 28–29

Williams, Lee, 28–30

workplace issues. *See* employment

Y

You Tube, 83–84

Z

Zeny (accounting app), 101